Gabriele Hannemann

SOULMATE GUIDEBOOK
(Twin Soul, Twin Flame, Dual Soul, Karmic Partner)

The greatest test of your life

FSC
www.fsc.org
MIX
Papier aus ver-
antwortungsvollen
Quellen
Paper from
responsible sources
FSC® C105338

Layout: Gabriele Hannemann
Translation: Tamara Koch, Zorana Bulat
Picture credits see at the back of the book

Manufactured and published by BoD – Books on Demand, Norderstedt.
ISBN: 9783752834420

Special remark:

Please note that all information and references in this book are based on sub-
jective spiritual experiences; no promises or guarantees of any kind are implied.
In particular, the advice in this book cannot replace necessary medical or th
rapeutic measures.

" *If this day was not your friend, it was at least your teacher.* "
(Unknown)

CONTENTS

INTRODUCTION

This guide is meant for all those who wish to learn more about the topic of soul connections and their learning tasks. Some members of the audience will certainly be able to identify with this text. Of course, everything I describe in this guide and my other books are merely recommendations.

Spirituality primarily teaches us to assume full responsibility for our own thoughts, emotions and actions. This guide does not describe generally applicable formulas, which dictate that things can only function this way. Instead, it contains suggestions to take a look at yourself. They can provide invaluable help if you are currently dealing with a difficult soul connection. In our own neediness, we often cannot see the forest for all the trees and we display strange behaviors toward our soul mate. Solving the entire mystery with the help of this guide will enable you to develop an understanding of the other person's behavior. Like in a mirror, you will learn to recognize yourself in him in order to heal your emotions and any obstructive patterns.

It is my wish to help people and to explain life's learning tasks in such a way that the human mind can grasp them. Once this has been accomplished, it can be quickly implemented in practice. This will make it easier to advance in those situations where you feel stuck apparently forever. Furthermore, conscious understanding will help you attract fewer repetitive situations and to heal and transform them in the best possible manner instead. Each individual is asked to walk the path of unique development. In a soul connection, it is important to have your own experiences. You need not be afraid of making mistakes. This is primarily about evolving and exploring certain features of your own personality.

There is no right or wrong, there are only non-judgmental soul experiences. Having personally experienced the connection with a soul mate, I was perfectly capable of gathering my own experiences with this issue. I have experienced many of the situations mentioned here or I observed them in other soul connections in order to learn more.

This revised Soul Mate Guide briefly summarizes and concisely outlines the most important issues of soul connections. Additional information and aspects are described in greater depth and detail in my books.

WHAT IF YOUR ROLES ARE SWITCHED?

From my consulting activities, I know some cases in which the described roles in a soul connection are completely reversed. In this case, you may be the male and your female soul mate withdraws in order to display the characteristics of the male soul mate described in this guide. The two of you may also be of the same gender.

However, for the story and development of the soul connection described in this guide, I assume that in the vast majority of cases the women will assume their role as the female and the men will assume their role of the male soul mate. If your own scenario is reversed or if you are in a same-gendered relationship, please interpret my descriptions by applying this fact to the situation. The role each partner assumes will be explained in the next section.

HOW DO I RECOGNIZE THAT I AM ASSUMING THE ROLE OF THE FEMALE SOUL MATE?

- If you are the one who wants to consciously address the circumstances of the soul connection;
- If you are the one who questions everything about this connection;
- If you are the one who approaches the other person time and again;
- If you are the one who always suffers whenever the other person withdraws;
- If you have the feeling you cannot be without the other person;
- If you are very impatient and the other person seems to have a lot of patience;
- If you keep questioning the other person's behavior time and again;
- If you are the one who can't let go of (release) the other person.

If you answered almost all of these questions with a "yes," you are most likely assuming the role of the female soul mate.

THE FIRST ENCOUNTERS WITH YOUR SOUL MATE

The topic of soul connections is very comprehensive. If you meet a soul mate during your lifetime, it frequently represents a huge challenge. In most cases, a lot of learning tasks are associated with this soul connection. This is not easy for the female soul mate, who often suffers more at the start of this encounter. Her suffering is caused by the male soul mate distancing himself from her quite quickly and by him acting contrary to what he told her.

Most people recognize each other in the form of love at first sight, which is mutual. Others only notice after a few encounters that there is strong love and familiarity.

Both are amazed that they tell so many private/intimate details from their life to a stranger, because there is a strong sense of intimacy. Both automatically recognize each other and have the feeling of already knowing the other person even though they have never met in the present lifetime.

In such scenarios, the two souls already know each other from one or several past lives. During such an encounter, it is not unusual to feel as if one looked into one's own eyes and was facing one's very own self.

AFTER THE FIRST ENCOUNTERS

The male soul mate often withdraws completely after the first encounter or after just a short while. He doesn't understand what has happened. He is very confused, since he has never experienced such intense emotions before.

The female soul mate experiences something very similar, yet she doesn't withdraw and would like to approach him. She is also confused but notices very quickly that this is the man of her dreams and her soul mate. She suffers greatly from his withdrawal and often senses his discomfort quite strongly – even across a great distance.

WHY DOES THE SOUL MATE WITHDRAW?

When two soul mates meet for the first time, enormous energies are exchanged at that moment. All it takes is being in the vicinity of the soul mate, because this energy exchange is of a spiritual and not a physical nature. As a result, these soul energies can even be perceived across great distances.

Once the initial contact with the soul mate has been established, she can feel his soul energy and his moods even across large distances. Physical characteristics may often manifest as side effects of the energy exchange between both individuals. These may include a nose itch, tingling in the earlobe, a ringing in the ear and the like. In most cases, there is a telepathic connection, which means that both know or feel what the other person is thinking or doing at the time. How strongly both soul mates can sense this depends on a person's individual development, maturity, the progress of his or her learning tasks and the strength of their connection.

In order to be able to handle this energy exchange more easily, both soul mates are allowed to energetically adjust to each other. Among others, this is the reason why such connections take time in the beginning. While both soul mates have very similar soul energies and structures, these energies are so familiar and resemble each other so much that the mind cannot make sense of it at first. Often, the many similarities and synchronicities will cause a clash, so that both soul mates may be completely stirred and confused. One of the souls most frequently reacts in the form of withdrawal (through unconscious recognition of the other familiar soul, often resulting in the manifestation of fear), while the other soul reacts with tremendous euphoria, quickly causing this soul to massively approach the other person energetically.

Based on this recognition, both soul mates develop an almost inevitable attraction, which is mostly also sexual in nature. It is almost impossible to escape. As a consequence, irregular encounters and recurring breaks will alternate, the energies of both souls can get used to each other, and they can make each other realize their learning tasks.

Since it is especially the male soul mate who is initially incapable of handling these energies, he quickly distances himself from his female soul mate. He doesn't understand what is happening and what he is dealing with. He does not believe that such a perfect woman exists, since he has only known someone like her from his dreams. By withdrawing from her, he can better sort himself out internally and regain a somewhat stable footing.
Often, he is still tied down in a partnership or marriage and starts "switching on" his reason and sense of responsibility again. More about this later.

Both soul mates quickly realize that they could be for each other exactly what they had always imagined their "dream partner" to be and that they would complement each other in every respect. The male soul mate pushes these thoughts away and is in denial even though he can feel it deep down. In contrast, the female soul mate wants to live this dream relationship and enjoy it as quickly as possible.

WHY DOES THE FEMALE SOUL MATE SUFFER FOR SO LONG IN THE BEGINNING?

The female soul mate will often suffer a lot in the beginning. Initially, she sustains the entire energy of the male soul mate as well and feels his unresolved patterns and suppressed emotions until he can gain momentum and start evolving. To some extent, she can determine how long she will suffer. Once she faces her own learning tasks instead of repressing or fighting them, her development will proceed and she will experience more and more lightness and self-healing. If she fights her learning tasks, the healing process of the soul can last a lot longer.

I cannot indicate specific time periods, since this can take anywhere from weeks, months and years to decades (in rare cases). To her, this time often feels like "hellish" soul agony, which is often caused by his complete withdrawal. This withdrawal activates the old and dark sides of her personality as well as lower patterns and brings them to the surface so she can look at them and heal them. If she didn't transform her old patterns, behaviors and dark sides, she would have a hard time evolving. Old unpleasant patterns, dark sides and lower behaviors include e.g. jealousy, self-doubt, the victim role, self-pity, self-hate, lack of self-esteem, impatience, compulsive controlling behavior, feelings of guilt, (co-)dependency, doubt, fear of wrong decisions, mistrust, conflicting behavior, fear of intimacy, fear of commitment, envy, vindictiveness, lechery, neediness, etc. These can exist consciously or subconsciously.

While the first encounters take place, the male soul mate is frequently still tied up in a marriage or partnership that has not been working for a long time, and he may have just forced himself to stay and deluded himself.

The relationship may also represent merely a habit or prestige that both would like to portray to the outside. It is also possible that the relationship is kept together by outside influence. One or both may stick to a promise that was made a long time ago. It is also often observed that the male soul mate clings to the security, joint care for the children or to a joint past. In this respect, he is deceiving himself, since he has enormous fear of losing everything and being seen as the "villain" in the circle of family and friends.

In such a marriage or partnership, I have often seen that the wife of the male soul mate is very dominant and they simply share the same place but no longer really "live together." It is also possible that both are already physically separated but that this separation hasn't been legally effected. In rare cases, the male soul mate will be single at the time of the first encounter, but he has an unresolved mother relationship or has not fully processed the relationship with an ex-partner. It is also possible that he gets involved with one or several women at a later date, which in reality has a certain, deeper meaning. I will explain later on why he does that.

THE ENERGY OF THE SOUL MATE

During the time the two soul mates do not see each other, there is nonetheless a very strong emotional tie between them through which many emotions or moods are consciously or unconsciously absorbed. Furthermore, many soul mates who have little contact in real life encounter each other at the dream level in order to continue fulfilling their learning tasks.

If he is unwell, she often notices that very quickly and is aware of it. As a result, she doesn't feel good either, because she hasn't learned to separate from his lower energies (lower energies are created e.g. by the fact that he forces himself not to approach her, even though his soul and heart would like to do it). In some cases, she doesn't feel consciously that he is unwell and wonders why she isn't feeling well, although there isn't always a reason for it.

If the reverse is the case and she is unwell, he often won't notice right away. In contrast to her, he doesn't notice it immediately that this has something to do with her, but the thinks that he is unwell because he is overworked or doesn't have a good day.

FEELING "HELLISH" SOUL AGONY

The worst situation occurs when one of the two partners starts missing the other. The other person feels this unconsciously and also starts missing the partner. This can be very painful for the female soul mate, since she also carries most of the energy for him in the beginning until he finally gains momentum. This mutual sense of longing becomes worse and more unbearable for her, since it is coming from both sides and is therefore basically doubled and tripled. This can become so bad for the female soul mate that it literally feels as if somebody is pulling the rug away from under her. For some it is so pronounced that they think of committing themselves to a mental institution or experience an actual death wish.

While these energies typically calm down over time, they can also return frequently until she has learned to handle them and to accept these feelings in order to derive a sense of self-worth and a primal sense of trust.

LEARNING TASKS OF THE FEMALE SOUL MATE

Primarily, she needs to learn patience and trust, because a soul mate often involves a long wait. These are the hardest learning tasks for her. If they were easy for her, they wouldn't be learning tasks.

She may also learn to accept his behavior and her situation with her soul mate. Love and transformation can only arise through unconditional acceptance. "Letting go with trust," as many people call it, does not mean to completely let go of the soul mate or to not believe in this special connection but to let go of the situation as it is with the knowledge that everything is right and that everything happens for a reason.

What she may let go of are the needy expectations, the waiting and the addiction to the soul mate, since these energies unconsciously repel the male soul mate instead of attracting him. The prerequisite for being able to release these lower energies is to first take them in and accept them. Nothing can be released and let go that wasn't previously accepted. The acceptance of such dark sides in oneself means moving more in the direction of self-love. If you don't love yourself, no confirmation from the outside or from the soul mate can occur.

Accepting the situation does not mean replacing the soul mate with the search for another partner in order to distract yourself from suffering or fears regarding the soul mate. That would simply mean that the learning tasks were not understood and that the problem would only be shifted.

If the Universe sends a new partner, he will likely represent a testing candidate who poses the same learning tasks as the actual soul mate.

For most female soul mates, it is very difficult to open up to a new man as long as there is still a strong fixation on the male soul mate. Meanwhile the male soul mate is more easily open to another woman in order to distract himself and to continue to suppress his feelings. Since this new woman isn't needy, it doesn't provoke any great fears in him. He doesn't get the feeling of being overrun, locked in, restricted or that he has to justify himself. Often the male soul mate projects emotions onto this new woman that he really feels for his female soul mate. This is not a conscious process for him. He is just too afraid of deluding himself with the female soul mate. In reality, he is deluding himself with the new woman. In most cases, he only realizes this much later and it serves his own evolution. He may learn something from the experience with another woman or open himself up to something he couldn't do yet with the female soul mate at this point in time due to her own learning processes. At the same time, he shows her subconsciously how she would have to tackle her learning tasks.

When the female soul mate meets a new man, she typically rejects him, since she wishes for a relationship and intimacy with her soul mate. However, in doing so she may overlook that she could also evolve through the new partner. Through him, she could also become better prepared for the relationship with the soul mate. Ultimately, this is about learning to discard your old patterns and to recognize and heal them based on a situation or event created by the Universe.

After all, neither of them knows what learning tasks are still to be mastered in order to make a harmonious life together in a soul mate relationship possible. It is no coincidence that initially another partner is sent to both of them.

A large part of the goals planned by the soul can also be achieved with other people before the soul mate relationship, if this was agreed with them on Earth. Otherwise, more painful tasks would have to be completed in the soul mate relationship.

It would be advisable for her not to compulsively get involved with another man only to feel validated, if she doesn't have any feelings for him. Among others, testing candidates can be recognized by the fact that you will develop feelings for them, even if your feelings for your soul mate are stronger and not even comparable in terms of the intensity.

If she has feelings for him, she needs to learn to have a man court her and to not immediately get involved in a relationship or become intimate with him (she needs to represent her own self-worth and femininity). If not even another man can make an effort to court her, since she won't allow it, how can her actual soul mate court her? Therefore, she will be sent as many new men as it takes for her to learn to be courted.

IN WHAT OR WHOM CAN SHE TRUST?

Walking the path into the soul connection means for her to learn to regain her primal sense of trust. The trust with which we were born and that we have lost over time, often due to our upbringing or other experiences and formative events.

Trusting the male soul mate from the very beginning is rarely possible, if he behaves in a very contradictory manner to her or if he is still lying to himself. In most cases, trust in the soul mate is only learned during the last phases that the soul mates go through. Instead, trust in the Divine Order (in the Creator of love for everything that IS) and inner guidance must first be regained and accepted.

The soul mate connection is agreed upon and arranged before this life in order to learn to receive guidance again and to feel oneself. Everything that happens between the soul mates is right the way it is and nothing can be forced and manipulated, since love always flows, is accepting and unconditional. Love can only arise through love and grow like a flower. Like will always attract like.

The more the female soul mate accepts things and lets them flow while trusting that everything is right the way it is and that everything will progress and take shape at the right time, the faster she will grow in her learning tasks. This way, the agreed soul objectives with the soul mate can be achieved more easily and more harmoniously. This is the only way for her to be able to learn to rest in herself, to take a look at herself and to evolve. The more she waits that he develops and approaches her, the longer her learning tasks will take and she will always look to the outside for blame or reasons instead of trusting in what she perceives inside in order to rest in herself and stay with her own learning tasks.

"Only once you have reached the source of your wisdom will you recognize the ridiculousness of space and time."
(Unknown)

SELF-LOVE

Self-love is the prerequisite for loving another person and for being loved. For we cannot find anything outside of ourselves that we haven't found within ourselves before. Loving ourselves means saying "yes to ourselves" unconditionally and to take good care of ourselves. To accept ourselves the way we are and to treat ourselves the way we would like to be treated by others. When the female soul mate meets the male, she starts by entering the waiting room and often forgets about herself. She keeps getting into this state of waiting time and again, fails to manage her everyday life for a long time and often has the feeling of being unable to live without him, since her entire life only revolves around him. This has little to do with self-love, but through these recurring situations she learns over time to increasingly develop her own self-worth and self-love. At some point she becomes aware of what she is doing, how much energy she is wasting and how much time goes by unused.

At the same time, this tiresome and needy waiting for the soul mate also means that she is putting off her own evolution.

If she starts to observe herself now and advances in her development, she will also recognize that he is a mirror (unconscious behavior of the male soul mate triggered by the unconscious patterns in her energy field) who wants to show her how she ultimately treats herself.

If she now changes the situation by using the so-called mirror in order to give to herself what she would like to receive from her soul mate or other people, she will increasingly find her way back again into her own strength. From then on, she will start to take care of herself more, to accept herself and therefore also her male soul mate and his behavior. This way, the development of both soul mates can advance more easily, because if she changes her energy and behavior, the male soul mate will unconsciously resonate.

" *Just because we are lacking a piece of happiness, we should not be deterred from enjoying everything else.*"
(Jane Austen)

THE OBSTACLES AT THE START OF THE PATH

If we didn't experience these obstacles and delays at the start of the path, change could not occur in the future. If we were to always behave in the same way, we would also attract repetition time and again.

It is for these reasons that we may experience obstacles, difficulties and often even stronger suffering in these soul connections. Only this way, based on such a connection, can deep-seated obstructive behavior patterns, dark sides and neediness be brought to the surface in a manner that wouldn't be possible with any other partner.

Based on partners we previously met, old structures and patterns are pre-activated. This already creates a kind of test run to show whether we are actually ready to look at our unresolved issues through this soul connection and are able to handle it.

When the soul energies clash, all the deep-rooted remaining and suppressed shares that are important for the advancement of our own personality come to the surface. This is significant for being able to heal them. It is very important that these feelings can rise and be activated, because otherwise we couldn't access these old patterns in order to change them.

If you encounter the soul connection but haven't gotten rid of your old behaviors and accepted and transformed your own dark sides, a harmonious or loving relationship cannot be lived. It is for these reasons that the energies of both soul mates are allowed to slowly get used to each other. This takes time so that each person can deal with his or her own dark sides and can heal them this way. If both got together right away or interacted too often and too closely, such a connection could possibly not be lived in this lifetime at all, since everything would go too fast. This would create enormous fears that could only rarely be overcome. It would be similar to prematurely opening a flower bud, so the blossom could probably not unfold its beauty.

In soul mates, too, the potential to be developed cannot unfold if they get together prematurely. The incomparable and intensive love both partners have for each other would pull the rug away from under their feet in such a way that neither of them would have any more confidence.

One of the two would break away sooner or later because of the excessive passion and intensity and would automatically push the other one away. For one of them (which is mostly the male soul mate), things get to intense and he cannot allow any more intimacy or contact. The other one (mostly the female soul mate) begins to question herself and her partner's love, is deeply hurt and doesn't want to put any more pressure on him or restrict him any further. This makes him totally insecure and he no longer knows how to behave. The outcome could be that nobody dares to contact the other, since either person's own life is turned upside down by overwhelming feelings resembling a rollercoaster ride due to the presence of the other soul mate. One of them doesn't want to be overrun while the other doesn't want to feel bad anymore, thinking that she is getting pushed away and abused.

Based on the addictive feelings both have for each other, they would massively lose themselves emotionally in the other person, since neither of them has learned to rest in themselves. Often, it is only by delaying this connection that setting boundaries, perceiving and feeling one's own inner voice and self-love can be learned.

If this should happen in extreme cases that one loses oneself in the other, it is very important to retreat and find oneself again or to deal with the issue internally. Based on your own withdrawal and dealing with the situation internally, you can recognize, allow, accept and therefore heal your own emotions regarding these issues. If these emotions weren't felt and healed, both might completely avoid and prevent contact in the future as a consequence, since one of them doesn't want to be tied down and the other doubts that there is love. Of course, once again it depends on the personal soul contracts that both agreed upon prior to this earthly life, because there are some soul mates that are very mature and aware when they meet. For these partners, things can also progress quickly and without many obstacles, but these are often people who already transformed many of their dark sides and old patterns in the past. So, if things don't advance so quickly in many soul mate relationships, this has a reason and one need not be upset about it.

Both energies are allowed to slowly get used to each other, which is why the path is obstructed by pebbles, stones or larger boulders in the beginning.

"The person who moved the mountain was the same person who started to carry away small stones."
(Chinese proverb)

WHY LETTING GO IS OFTEN SO HARD FOR THE FEMALE SOUL MATE

In most cases, it is difficult for her, since she focuses on release instead of acceptance. Love doesn't know release, just acceptance. The more she practices to accept the situation, the behavior and the decisions of the male soul mate (who is also undergoing his own personal development), the easier it will become for her. However, the more she focuses on letting him go, to suppress him and to ban him from her head and her heart, the more resistance she will build, which is what she basically DOESN'T want.

Think for yourself! Do you want this connection with your soul mate at all? Do you wish to experience these emotions harmoniously? Then it will be important to accept even the unpleasantness to facilitate healing and transformation.

Don't fight him or this connection anymore and DON'T question what you perceive inside but allow it. Don't get confused by his behavior or what others are saying and don't believe your own self-deception but listen and trust in your inner voice. Or why do you think you received a feeling, an inner voice and an intuition from God?

At the very moment you accept things that appear externally or internally, love can happen. From this moment on, everything begins to flow. The moment you accept everything the way it is, you will also trust.

Of course, nobody claims that acceptance is easier than letting go, but if it were easy, it would hardly be necessary to learn it. All things that are hard for us in our lives may be learned so that development can occur.

It can also easily happen that you get very angry when you truly and actually accept the whole issue with him. However, this is good and right, because only when an unpleasant situation is accepted can suppressed or repressed anger, disappointment or sadness come to the surface. This is how you recognize your authentic acceptance. During this process, it is very important to accept these emotions and to feel them completely. It would be best for you to find an outlet for them, such as the following examples:

- *Take a pillow and punch it.*
- *Scream in your car or into a pillow as loudly as you can.*
- *Join a gym in order to vent your aggression and anger through exercise.*
- *Have a day of grieving, which is best done with a*
- *sappy romance movie in order to better activate and allow suppressed sadness.*

MASTERING EVERYDAY LIFE

For most female soul mates, it is a great challenge to get back to an orderly and normal everyday life after encountering their soul mate. In most cases, she is mentally so busy with him that she cannot focus on her work or anything else in her daily life. She wakes up with thoughts of him in the morning and goes to bed with them at night.

This is another learning task for her – to rest with herself and to stay in the present to advance her tasks and projects and to invest her energy in herself, her work and her everyday responsibilities. She best learns this as the soul connection is delayed. In the beginning, she loses a lot of energy, since her thoughts only revolve around him: What is he doing, what is he thinking, why does he withdraw, when will he get in touch, when will we meet again, when will we have a relationship?

If she doesn't figure out by herself that this distraction and lack of being centered robs her of a lot of energy, she will automatically get to a point at which she actually breaks down or comes close to it. From this learning task arises the opportunity to recognize her self-worth and to grow into it step by step. Once she has succeeded, she will have realized that it was important to recognize her own life, her self-delusions and self-deceptions and to find herself again. From that moment on, she begins to experience joy in her life again, to understand the meaning of this encounter and to perceive and accept it as a gift.

If she has recognized this encounter as a gift, she will find composure and joy again in the things she is doing at the present time. Of course, it can happen occasionally that she falls into a small hole, but in most cases she will now be able to handle it more easily, and she has learned not to dig any deeper if she is already inside of such a hole but to climb out and master such situations.

Of course, everyday life and its tasks would be much easier to handle, if the male soul mate were already at her side. However, if that were the case, she would not be able to access her unhealed emotions and hidden patterns and no real evolution would take place.

TRUE LOVE OR DEPENDENCY?

True love can never be found on the outside but only on the inside. If you haven't found love and validation (self-worth) in yourself yet, your own patterns will repeat in the relationship with a new partner. You will experience the same injuries as in the past in very similar form until you have learned to find and allow love inside yourself instead of looking for it or demanding validation on the outside. You can then continue and live your power games, expectations and demands with other training partners. This will only change once you begin to give to yourself everything that you would so love to receive from your soul mate. Through the encounter with your soul mate you are already realizing what is missing inside of you. Once you begin to give to yourself what you want from others, healing can occur and the corresponding repetitive patterns will be a thing of the past.

These are the reasons why your counterpart serves as a mirror. Through his behavior, your partner will unconsciously allow you to recognize existing patterns in yourself so that you can resolve and heal them. Based on this healing work, a soul connection will begin to flow again more easily in order to also master the remaining learning tasks.

LEARNING TASKS OF THE MALE SOUL MATE

The learning tasks of the male soul mate are primarily geared toward eliminating his heavy mind focus and to act more in tune with his emotions than his reason.

He feels that these supernatural or extraordinary circumstances happening due to the encounter with the female soul mate are unrealistic, since he cannot comprehend them through reason. He is allowed to open up to the insight that this female soul mate is exactly his matching complement and that she can offer him everything from a human standpoint he ever dreamed of. Even though he senses this somehow, he doesn't want to realize it and withdraws, he starts to think and behave very strangely. Over time, the male soul mate becomes more aware and can therefore slowly open up to the female soul mate and get somewhat closer to her. In addition, he may have to learn to recognize his own self-delusion and to part with old views or things that burden him. Among others, this can also be an existing relationship or marriage, if he stays with it out of self-constraint, for security or out of habit, or if he clings to the past for fear of being lonely.

This is not about leaving a harmonious or happy marriage or relationship but to actually detach from burdening old belief patterns and conditions. However, this can also be a longstanding relationship or marriage, if both partners are only deluding themselves.

Often, such relationships are only kept together by the couple's children or the parents themselves do not wish to separate because of the children. In these cases, the parents often overlook diseases or deficits in the children that are created by their parents' constant arguments or because they send out negative energies. Children unconsciously sense what is really going on and they automatically react to or mirror the parents' behavior through their own dissatisfaction, hyperactivity, irritability or illness, when the parents do not listen to their soul but cling to old paradigms or outdated ideas.

Of course, most children don't want their parents to separate, but now it must be examined exactly what would be easier for oneself and the children and their further path.

Either they suffer a lot from their parents' many arguments and notice that they do not love each other anymore or they adopt the same behaviors in their later love life. They may also fight frequently with their partner or unintentionally look for such an argumentative partner time and again, or they don't separate either because of their own children.

This way, children may not truly be able to walk their own path, because a pattern could be created that may persist across multiple generations until it is resolved and healed. In addition, nobody knows whether these children planned before this lifetime to learn through this precise experience of the parents' separation and to develop as a result.

There have also been cases in which the existing family life of some people became more harmonious again and the love for the current partner became stronger because of the soul mate. Here it depends on what is written in the soul contracts of these people. The primary reason why two soul mates meet in life is that your life can be evaluated, since the soul mate presents you with a mirror and this connection reveals all deceptions and self-deceptions.

"Reason can tell us what we should refrain from, but the heart can tell us what we have to do."
(Joseph Joubert)

As soon as the male soul mate has learned trust and honesty toward himself, his female soul mate and other people, he will understand why things in his life proceed the way they do and why he encountered his female soul mate.

Soul mates frequently meet when one of the partners or even both are still unavailable. The Universe has designed it this way, so that these soul mates meet during a time when their marriages or relationships have been in crisis for some time and they can no longer mentally grow with their partner or when they have not fully processed the relationship with an ex-partner. If the soul mates were to meet when they are fully available, the corresponding learning tasks could not be understood and mastered.

A person can't help who he or she falls in love with, because this is an uncontrollable event that occurs unconsciously. You are always interested in a person or fall in love with him or her when your Higher Self (the soul) notices that something can be learned through this other person or that you can personally develop through him or her.

There is also the possibility that the two soul mates cling to their existing marriage or relationship but cheat on their partner. This is a sign that the existing relationship has gone dormant or is only maintained for various other reasons. If this were a happy relationship, no outsider could get in.

Often, you stick to material things or are too considerate of others, and ultimately you punish yourself, since you are unable to make decisions due to many fears controlling you. "What would the others say?" or "What would I think of myself?" or "How will this continue?" etc., etc.

In order to not delay the learning tasks any further, you must also make sure not to get sexually involved with the male soul mate as long as he is still in a relationship. (By relationship, we mean what was agreed upon between the partners and not what was established on paper.)

This can help prevent additional negative karma, which would otherwise be created by getting intimately involved with the unavailable soul mate. Getting involved with an unavailable soul mate could simultaneously create dishonesty in our energy field, since he possibly lies to his partner. This is absolutely not recommended, since your relationship would being based on insincerity, which could also continue throughout your entire relationship. For the person who cheats on his or her partner, it would also become more difficult because of such actions to attract honesty to his or her life.

Primarily for the female soul mate, it is important to remain in her femininity and her self-worth, which would be prevented by an affair with the soul mate. This could further delay a fulfilling relationship or the planned soul objective, since she would act against her own learning tasks by agreeing to an affair.

BEHAVIORS TOWARD THE MALE SOUL MATE SHE SHOULD AVOID IF SHE IS STILL NEEDY

- *Under no circumstances should she exert pressure on the male soul mate or make him choose, since he could otherwise withdraw even more. It is very important to give him the time he needs for his development and for overcoming his fears.*
- *She should not fall into a depression or have doubts when his behavior is often contrary to what he says. This behavior is natural if he is afraid of his overly strong feelings for her.*
- *She should not give up on herself only because he does not approach her that quickly, because he also needs his time for developing and maturing, just like she does.*
- *She should not agree to physical intimacy as long as the male soul mate is still in a relationship, because this would only delay and complicate things. With such behavior, she can't attract lightness and honesty.*
- *She should not immediately judge the situation with him but stay in a state of observation.*

Other behaviors she should avoid are described in greater detail in my books.

QUESTIONS AND ANSWERS

HOW TO RECOGNIZE THE SOUL MATE?

In most cases, if you entered a special connection with a soul mate, both partners in the relationship have important tasks to master. Both have prepared a special soul plan as well as an intensive or unique connection based on which the individual can evolve strongly. In this special connection, you can often recognize the following characteristics:

- *You can't stop thinking about this person, even if you have been out of touch for years.*
- *You think about him for months or years, every time you get up in the morning and when you go to bed at night.*
- *You both experience synchronicities, e.g. you have the same interests, you like the same objects, you have the same tastes, the same hobbies, the same living situation, the same experiences, the same personal traits, the same physical features, the same events in life, etc.*
- *You do or plan the same things at the same time without the other one knowing about it.*
- *You have a telepathic connection with each other.*
- *You feel how the other one is doing, even if he or she isn't close by.*
- *I have also often observed that you may have a friend for whom the apparently same thing is happening almost simultaneously.*

WHY DOES SHE FIRST GO THROUGH THIS "HELLISH" SOUL AGONY?

If there is still old karma from one or several past lives between the two, this soul agony may be experienced to resolve (balance) the karma between both partners. At the same time, old dark sides, ego structures and patterns are brought to light, which allows you to become aware of them and resolve them. Furthermore, this isn't really "hellish" soul agony but old, unhealed wounds and unconscious patterns and pain from the past, which soon come to the surface based on the encounter of the soul mates. All of this wasn't reviewed and healed in the past.

When these old, lower structures break out, our ego suggests that it doesn't want to heal these old issues and therefore perceives them as very painful. Since we don't really like pain and unpleasant things, we push them away whenever they get activated based on the frequent experience of rejection, or we don't want to get confronted by them.

This exactly starts the vicious circle and the actual learning tasks get drawn out. Based on the suppression of these emotions and these unpleasant feelings, we procrastinate the whole matter for us.

Just like the male soul mate suppresses and pushes his strong emotions away toward the female soul mate, she also often pushes the negative feelings, which are often associated with fear of loss, lack of self-worth or fear or rejection, far away from her instead of accepting and healing them.

It is very important to deal with unpleasant feelings and emotions and to voluntarily pay attention to them. Once they come up, the quickest and simplest way to access them is to accept them, to experience them voluntarily, which means feeling and therefore healing them. As a result, you look your fears directly in the eye. The more they are pushed away, the more frequently and vehemently they will have to come up, since your own soul wants to finally heal them in order to be able to evolve.

Unhealed aspects, patterns and issues of built-up karma from this and past lives can combine into a mixture which is felt as truly painful and can often be experienced as "hellish" soul agony.

If there is still karma between both soul mates that is unresolved or needs to be healed, the encounter in this life provides them with the best opportunity to finally heal it. It is recommended that both pay attention not to create new karma with each other, e.g. through dishonesty, secret affairs or acts of revenge. This would not help in alleviating the karmic burden, since more is added (if you want to eliminate debt, it isn't recommendable either to take out more loans or make new debt). This could further delay the healing of both soul mates and the achievement of this connection's soul objective. This makes the connection even more complicated than it already is.

While this sounds very painful and complicated, it is normal that we are tested time and again on our path to finding ourselves. Each individual decides for him-or herself how long this soul pain will last and how honest he or she is and remains to him- or herself on this path to finding oneself. From the moment when the learning tasks and issues come up from the inside and are accepted instead of rejected, the pain gets less and healing can finally take place.

WHY DOES SHE KEEP FALLING INTO THIS HOLE?

This is part of the learning tasks. Only based on these tasks will she be able to learn to handle the situation and to have an easier time staying centered. The faster she learns to manage these emotional relapses and to accept them, the faster they will pass.

WHAT CAN YOU DO WHEN DOUBTS CREEP IN AGAIN?

When you experience these doubts again as to whether you be-long together (and these doubts will definitely recur, since they are tests designed by the Universe), you can do the following:

Ask the Universe, the angels or God for help and a clear sign for yourself, **for example:**

- *Ask for a sign for yourself if you really belong together.*
- *Ask for a sign for yourself if it is worthwhile keeping up hope with regard to this connection.*
- *Ask for a sign in order to become attentive to things that are important to you in this respect and to be able to also recognize these signs.*
- *Ask for a sign for yourself to see if you are still with your harmonious soul plan.*
- *Or ask the angels to guide you back to your harmonious soul path.*

It is even more advisable to not issue a request but communi-cate gratitude for sending these signs instead. You can do this in the following form:

"Thank you for giving me this sign or another."

Then we don't signal neediness or strong deprivation, but we al-ready radiate gratitude with the certainty and trust that we will safely receive the sign and are grateful to receive it. This is one of the strongest possibilities for attracting the things we want. Too frequent and too intensive – especially needy – pleas for a wish to be fulfilled can cause us to radiate the energy of depri-vation. As a result, we would suggest to the Universe that we wish for something we don't have, and we get stuck with this energy of deprivation. Of course, you can ask for different signs more often, but – as I mentioned before – I can only recommend to release this request or wish right away or to send it filled with the energy of abundance and full of gratitude.

WHERE AND WHEN TO RECEIVE THE "SIGNS"?

In most cases, the signs are sent in such a manner that they are recognizable on the outside, except when you already have deeper access to your Higher Self (your soul). In this case, information and messages can show up internally as clairsentience or be seen with the so-called third eye.

However, at the beginning of this journey, most people receive their signs externally, e.g. in the form of license plates, street signs, TV, radio, posters, book titles, newspaper clippings, etc. Anything that is written, pictures or auditive information – sometimes also with other people we observe in our own environment – can show us these signs.

Examples:

- You are thinking about your soul mate, and suddenly a song plays on the radio that you connect with him.
- His name is mentioned on the radio or on TV.
- A show on TV or a song on the radio tells exactly the story of the two of you, or a person is shown who greatly resembles your soul mate.
- You are constantly passed by cars that carry his initials on the license plate.
- You see a gigantic poster with his name or something you always connect with him (e.g. a crown, a celebrity, an animal, a certain object or symbol).

Other types of signs and how they work exactly is described in greater detail in my book entitled:

"The Truth About Soulmates (Twin Souls, Twin Flames, Dual Souls, Karmic Partners) Part 1: Phases - Heavenly connection with infernal anguish ISBN: 9783752834420."

WHEN A RELATIONSHIP IS THE GOAL

When both have mastered their learning tasks, they are automatically reunited by the Universe. The attraction between them now consists of harmonious energies, so that they can finally live in a relationship. In most cases, the female soul mate has learned the necessary learning tasks faster and the male soul mate lags a little behind with his own learning tasks.

Now the female soul mate can be patient again without taking a seat in the "waiting room." This means that she normally continues her life with joy, because she has already largely learned the patience and the trust. She recognizes this because all of a sudden she has much more of both in many other areas of her life. At that point, her neediness will have disappeared and she barely feels any longing emotions anymore.

At the end of the most important learning tasks, both soul mates will become aware what exactly they have learned through the other person. Each of them will have also settled their private situations. Only then will they be able to attract each other again harmoniously.

It is for this reason that I recommend to everybody to be grateful if the reunion is a little delayed, because if both were to enter a relationship quickly, the energies would often be too extreme. Both would probably separate just as quickly and suddenly again. It happens frequently that multiple such relationship and separation phases occur (on-off relationship).

In such a case, the learning topics are even more extreme and mostly also associated with many power games. If this is the case, I urge you to be cautious to avoid landing in a mental hospital based on the excessively fast development with the most vehemently emerging emotions.

EXPERIENCING A HARMONIOUS SOUL MATE RELATIONSHIP

If both have mastered their learning tasks and nobody resumes certain old patterns, the desired partnership can finally be enjoyed. It doesn't compare to any other relationship. Both appreciate each other with all their hearts and have so much love for each other that they will live a completely new and fulfilled life. Both have also increased their energy and are jointly walking the path of spirituality/awakening. They can offer each other what they could only dream of before. Each will automatically read the other's every wish from their eyes. They will support and help each other in every respect and will be able to jointly achieve things in life each one would have never attained alone.

This also includes the issues of profession and vocation, because both can achieve much more in a joint partnership and be more successful in their profession/vocation, provided they have initiated the necessary steps before (established themselves) and did not allow themselves to get distracted from their task by the other.

Both will be faced with new learning tasks in the relationship, which will now become simpler and more harmonious, since the two will consciously work on them together and encourage each other, instead of running away from the soul mate in fear.

Both soul mates may also jointly produce or bring into the world new goals and projects. These are often partnerships that can last very long or even an entire lifetime. In this case, you can also serve as a great role model for others as to how you interact in a partnership. This would also mean a great contribution to mankind, because it will help other people evolve more quickly, to mature and to also raise their energies more easily.

WHEN THE PATH OF DEVELOPMENT IS THE GOAL

If both souls have chosen the path of development without a relationship, the female soul mate may often wish for this relationship nonetheless. If this need did not exist, she couldn't look at her learning tasks. As a result, she wouldn't be able to transform her neediness, impatience and her lack of self-esteem.

One thing is definitely clear:

If she mastered her learning tasks in terms of her soul mate, she will not be sad or discontent in the end if things don't lead to a joint partnership. The path was worth taking for her newly acquired abilities and her great development alone. And who knows? Maybe another soul mate will show up with whom a relationship is in the soul contracts? Since she learned a few things through her first soul mate and has already evolved, she doesn't need to repeat the things she already learned with the new soul mate. Then the relationship can often advance more quickly and more easily and a harmonious partnership can be achieved and experienced.

HOW DO YOU RECOGNIZE THAT CERTAIN LEARNING TASKS ARE CONCLUDED?

If both have worked on and balanced their mutual karma, both partners will no longer feel resonance in certain situations in which they would have reacted extremely or in a special manner in the past. For example, if there is still a negative resonance to the other person, something hasn't yet been recognized, accepted and healed internally. If both still have resonance to each other, even though they believe it's over, the learning tasks are either not yet finished or a relationship may still be the goal after all.

WHEN WILL HE APPROACH HER?

Each of the soul mates will ultimately help determine how quickly the other soul mate will approach him or her. The faster you accept and master your learning tasks, the faster the other person will go into resonance and the repetitive patterns will stop.

According to my own observations, both have certain learning tasks to master before they can attract each other again. Often it will be she who starts looking at certain issues and patterns and healing them before he can even get going. This has to do with the fact that it is usually also she who would like to advance things and who works more consciously on her own development than he does. He often doesn't even know that these are learning tasks.

Therefore, it is also the female soul mate, who may invest much strength and patience into her own learning tasks so that things can advance a bit at all. The male soul mate will often catch up later, since he is busy suppressing things for some time. This enables her to deal with her patterns. Once she has mastered certain learning tasks, he will receive an impulse at the soul level in order to approach her a bit again.

If he approaches her a bit and she relapses into her old patterns again, the male soul mate will most likely withdraw from her again. This can happen as often as it takes for her to learn not to relapse into her hold patterns.

If both have made good progress in their development, it can also happen that she no longer relapses into certain pattern, but he withdraws again nonetheless or keeps up his withdrawal.

If this is the case, she often feels that he no longer suppresses his feelings for her but that his fears are still keeping him from acting. However, if she no longer relapses into certain old patterns, she can handle the situation in a much more relaxed manner, since she feels exactly what's going on and she has already learned to be patient. If both have chosen the relationship in their soul contracts, he will approach her as soon as he has faced and overcome his fears.

IF THE MALE SOUL MATE GETS INVOLVED WITH OTHER WOMEN

In this case, she is allowed to learn how to handle this situation. At the same time, this means that she has another learning program to master, i.e. managing or accepting her upcoming jealousy in order to be able to heal it. Her soul shows her that she hasn't fully attained self-worth and trust.

His learning task in all of this is to recognize that he may look as much and as long for other women with the same qualities as he wants (he does this unconsciously) but that he won't find them. This is the only way for him to understand and learn that this connection is so intense and unique and to learn to accept it at the same time.

In most cases, he searches unconsciously – or sometimes also consciously – for proof that he isn't crazy. While he won't find this proof, he can only become aware of it if he tries – and the female soul mate will benefit from this.

At this point, I have observed that he often likes to select or attract women who either very much resemble the female soul mate or have very similar personality traits. In a lot of cases, he will delude himself, but he needs this to recognize and find his own truth. This other woman (frequently a testing candidate) is maybe very interesting in the beginning, but over time the relationship with her deteriorates due to a lack of interest and decreasing feelings and intensity.

The fact that he gets involved with another woman may be very painful for the female soul mate, since she thought he would finally make his way to her. However, this will help her recognize that both are not yet ready for this intense connection.

This topic is part of her learning tasks of acceptance and self-worth again. If he didn't have this experience with the other woman, he wouldn't be able to find out that his soul mate is ultimately the right one and his matching complement.

Note:

Regardless of whether it's a karmic partner, soul mate, twin soul or twin flame – the learning tasks in these soul connections are typically the same. The more you fixate on what "he" or "she" might or should be, the further you could move away from your own learning tasks.

It is important that you remain with yourself and assume full responsibility for your own tasks, because personal evolution is the highest soul objective. Of course, when recognizing your own self it can be helpful to know what type of union this is, so you have an easier time handling it. But in the end, it is always love that connects two people, regardless of whether both have a relationship as the goal in their soul contract or the path of evolution.

Best of luck in mastering your learning tasks!

Yours,
Gabriele Hannemann

"If you can't succeed today,
Forced actions cannot be the way!
If you don't yet comprehend,
Mature some more to further mend!
What today is still concealed
may tomorrow be revealed!"

(BO YIN RA)

This Soulmate Guidebook was a summary and reading sample of the books by Gabriele Hannemann >>THE TRUTH ABOUT SOULMATES (Twin Souls, Twin Flames, Dual Souls, Karmic Partners)<<,which are published in German.

CONTACT:

Those who'd like to write to me may use the following address or send an email (please avoid manually written documents to ensure that I can read everything right):

Gabriele Hannemann
Postfach 1127
85749 Karlsfeld
Germany

if you want to write me an email:
info@gabriele-hannemann.de

If you liked my book and found it useful, it would be kind of you to recommend it to others, for example, write a review at Amazon so that other people can easily find it. If you have a Facebook or Instagram account, or even your own Youtube channel, it would be great to share it there. The more people get to find help and support, the greater the chance of encouraging a worthwhile contribution to their personal development and also progress in their soulmate relationships.

I have a Youtube channel as well; however, the videos there are in German language. In the future, kindly supported by others, I hope to be able to get my explanations on the topic of soul relationships translated into English subtitles. If interested, you can take a look there anyway:

www.youtube.com/user/Gabrielehannemann

You'll also find a lot of texts and contributions related to topics focusing on spirituality and soulmates on my website, which could turn out to be useful to you. With the help of Google Tool (scroll down to the bottom of the page), my Website can be translated into any desired language. I'm looking forward to you there:
www.gabriele-hannemann.de
(Personal consultations can only be done in German though.)

There will be new parts of my books in English following
in the future!

BIOGRAPHY

Since the age of 13, Gabriele Hannemann has been dealing with spirituality. With the knowledge she has gained over the years as a spiritual life coach, she supports many people in finding their own personal soul path again.

The focus of her work is in the comprehensive area of "soul connections." Based on her own experience, she has studied the typical characteristics that mark the relationships between karmic partners, soul mates, twin souls and twin flames. Furthermore, her consultations have supplied a wealth of growing knowledge that also provided clear external confirmation on the topic.

To make the challenging situations of soul connections more easily bearable for those affected by them, Gabriele Hannemann published her first soul mate guide on the Internet a few years ago. The gratitude of many people that subsequently literally poured in prompted her to continue communicating her knowledge in detail in her book entitled "The Truth About Soul Mates (Twin Souls, Twin Flames, Dual Souls, Karmic Partners)." You can find a wealth of information and reports on the topic of soul

loving greetings from Munich (Germany)

Yours,
Gabriele Hannemann

Author, Specialist and Coach for soulmates, twin souls, dual souls and spiritual consultancy.

NOTES:

The Truth About
Soulmates
(Twin Souls, Twin Flames, Dual Souls, Karmic Partners)

Heavenly connection with infernal anguish

Part 1: Phases

ISBN: 9783752833539
(Gabriele Hannemann)